A GOOD MAN

JOHNA PASSARO

TABLE OF CONTENTS

Part I

To each there comes in their lifetime,
A special moment,
When they are figuratively tapped on the shoulders
And offered the chance to do a very special thing,
Unique to them and fitted to their talents.

Winston Churchill

JOHNA PASSARO

-1-
The Facts

The strongest men weaken
And the wisest men error

Mahatma Ghandi

There is a good man who sits in jail.

I know him well.

Let me correct that.

For a few years, I knew him well.

I believe I still do.

I am not claiming he is innocent, because he is not.

I am claiming he is good, because he is.

It is naïve to define a good man as one who has never done a bad thing in his life.

We all have.

I don't know if the value of one's life is the accumulation of all the good one has done minus all the bad.

Or should you throw out the best and worst actions of one's life and just look at the core?

Or does one just use the simple "Would I invite him over to Sunday dinner?" test to see on which side of the fence a person falls?

But what I do know is if the universe were to separate the good men from the bad, the man of whom I am speaking would undoubtedly fall on the side of the good - as he would pass on all of the above tests.

I am sure of that.

I am also sure if we all were to be judged simply by the worst thing we have ever done in our lives, not a soul who has ever lived would seem to have any redeeming value at all.

I tell this story, not to overlook or ignore the pain of this man's victims, for that pain is very real and is most definitely permanent.

But rather I tell it in hopes of letting this man know he is an extremely valuable human being who has made a difference in my life.

I hope this knowledge will be the kindle which keeps the fire of his goodness burning.

That would be very fitting, as many years ago he lit a fire of goodness inside of me.

Sometimes good people make very bad mistakes - or choices - whichever you prefer.

When good people make bad mistakes, they know it.

It bothers them.

Right down to their core.

For them to live with that knowledge is their lifelong torture.

For them to confuse this torture with their goodness as a person would be a mistake.

Good people sometimes do bad things.

But they are certainly still quite capable of producing more goodness in this world.

A world that so badly needs it.

Edmund Burke said: "The only thing necessary for the triumph of evil is for good men to do nothing."

For if every good man who has ever done a bad thing were to stop contributing good to this world, this world would soon be devoid of any good in it at all.

And evil would triumph.

And I just can't let that happen.

- 2 -
INSIDE OUT

If there is a magic in telling a story
The formula seems to lie solely
In the aching urge of the writer
To convey something he feels is
Important to the reader.

John Steinbeck

There are times in your life when you run into someone who winds up making a huge difference in your life.

In how you think, how you act, who you are and who you've become.

And despite time or their absence, a piece of them continue to live inside of you.

The good man of whom I speak… his name is Bill.

Bill has been such a person to me.

He was the first boss I ever had in my life.

The best boss I ever had in my life.

Bill was my Secretariat of bosses.

It's been thirty-one years and no one has even come close.

I have only seen Bill a handful of times over those thirty-one years.

I was a kid back when I first met Bill.

I am a man now.

In between, I have lived a lot of life.

My life has bounced between the extremes of exhilarating and excruciating – sometimes in the very same day.

It has taken me more than six years to learn how to keep my life at least 1% more exhilarating than excruciating at any given moment.

But no matter where I have ever been in my life's cycle, the impact Bill made on me and my life has always been quite evident to me.

A good man has that impact on you.

He helps you in the good times, as well as the bad.

When Bill was my boss, I saw him every day.

And I never told him how I felt about him.

I haven't seen Bill in over eight years.

To let him know what he has meant to me is now a driving force in my life.

I can't explain why.

Maybe it is because I believe when someone impacts your life, it is important to let that person know they made a difference.

And I didn't back then.

I only hope the reason why I didn't tell Bill how I felt back then was so I would tell him on the day he really needs to hear it.

Today.

They say writers write when they have something on their inside they must get out.

I agree with that.

I liken it to a beach ball that is held under water.

Eventually it needs to be released.

- 3 -
STILL LIVING

Bees have to move very fast to stay still.

David Foster Wallace

My life is different now than what it was when I worked for Bill.

Not better, nor worse.

Just drastically different.

I embrace that.

For the last six years, BettyJane and I have been caregivers to our daughter Jessica, who in 2009 lost oxygen to her brain for six minutes.

It is amazing what just six minutes can do to your world.

Jessica now requires around the clock care.

Over the last 2,190 days, either BettyJane or I have literally been by Jess's side at every given moment.

BettyJane and I are both desperately doing all we can to improve her life.

.1% at a time.

It is excruciating.

It is within this excruciation that I have found an exhilaration for life.

I have traded the hustle and bustle of my prior life for minimization.

Optimization.

Organization.

Appreciation.

Maximization.

For meaning.

I have spent a significant amount of time reflecting on my life - analyzing, uncovering, organizing and trying to make sense of my life's events.

To understand what truly is important in life.

I have recently started to practice 'stillness' as a way of tapping into my soul - to listen and to connect to my inner being.

To find answers.

To find answers to questions I never imagined I would ever have had to ask.

But I do.

In these stillness sessions I just sit completely still, clear my mind and allow my inner voice to speak to me.

I find that during these sessions, what is communicated to me seems to come from the source of life's great plan.

A plan in which I initially never quite understand.

A plan at which I marvel when I pay attention to coincidences that start occurring in my life.

Stillness has become the genesis of small miracles in my life.

It is my soul's magnetic compass.

Stillness points me in the right direction and pulls me onto the right path.

I have learned to blindly travel on whatever path it directs me.

Sometimes the path on which stillness directs me is a public road, lit with a bright sun.

Other times the path is in the woods at night, as I travel alone in the dark.

I have learned wherever the path is, whether public or private, in the light or in the dark, it is the exact path I need to travel in order to fulfill my role in this unique journey which we all call life.

If Bill were able to hear the chatter in my mind, he would know how often I have thought about him recently.

But obviously he can not.

So there is this gap in my perception of communicating with Bill, and the reality of the matter.

I have often thought about writing or visiting Bill, but something in my life always takes priority.

The proverbial beach ball gets to the surface, ready to explode out of the water, only to be pushed back down by the circumstances of my life.

Even though I know I should use theses circumstances as a catalyst to express my feelings, I have used them as an excuse not to.

Days have turned into weeks.

And weeks have turned into months.

It has been nearly a year and I have yet to communicate with Bill in his time of need.

What is inside of me has yet to come out.

In the creative world, they say the more resistance you face completing a project, the more important it is to your soul's development.

That would explain things.

One of my goals after my daughter's tragedy is to make more good than bad come from her situation.

To be the pebble of kindness dropped into the ocean of life.

That causes a ripple.

Which creates a wave.

Which floods the world - with love.

I just don't know what it is I should do?

- 4 -
CHARADES

When a man's willing and eager,
The gods join in.

Aeschylus

I imagine the rules of communication between our subconscious mind and our conscious mind are similar to that of a game of charades.

Where our subconscious mind needs to act out the clues for the word or phrase it wants to convey to our conscious mind.

Without having the luxury of verbal communication, the subconscious mind gets to use its physical body, nature, instead.

I imagine this game of charades goes on under the surface of our awareness until our conscious mind gets close to solving our subconscious mind's clue.

I believe it is then that we are sent a feeling.

I believe this feeling either rises above the surface of normal everyday life and gets us to act, or as it gets to the surface, we push it back down.

I believe when this feeling emerges, it is extremely important that we pay close attention to two things – to the coincidences occurring in our lives and to our encounters with the spectacular beauty of nature.

For that is where I believe the answers will reside.

In Anne Lamott's book, "Bird by Bird" she writes:

"There is ecstasy in paying attention.

Where you see in everything the essence of holiness."

This "essence of holiness" is often shown to us in the beauty of nature.

We all have had that momentary glimpse into the beauty of nature - a spectacular sunrise, a moving sunset, snow magically covering trees.

Most of us peak for a few seconds, marvel, and then go on with our daily lives.

In essence, pushing the beach ball back down under the water's surface.

I have learned it is important to do more.

I have learned to let nature's magical moments fuel my spirit and guide my actions.

Henry David Thoreau said: "I believe that there is a subtle magnetism in nature, which, if we unconsciously yield to it, will direct us aright."

I believe when the beauty of nature stops us in our life, it is vitally important for us to take the time to reflect on our life.

For this is when, in life's game of charades, I believe the conscious mind has solved our subconscious mind's clues.

It is during this brief time when we pause to take in nature's beauty that our heart and soul become one.

It is then coincidences in our lives will emerge.

I believe these coincidences are not merely coincidences, they are clues.

It is our soul banging on the door that separates the realm of our conscious from our subconscious worlds.

It is where our soul resides.

This banging produces a perfect combination of truly "knowing" and "feeling" inside of us.

This "knowing feeling" is the ultimate sensation one can feel on this earth.

It is the sensation that one is exactly where one is meant to be at this given moment in one's life.

I have the "knowing feeling" right now.

It is as if my conscious mind is yelling out "sounds like" as my subconscious mind is tugging on its ear.

- 5 -
NATURES MAGNETIC PULL

Beauty is natures operating instructions.
Nature slows you down
To appreciate the moment
By connecting what is the deeper part of your soul.

Louis Schwartzberg

There is a natural phenomenon that takes place twice a year in New York City called the "Manhattanhenge", a phrase coined by the great scientist Neil deGrasse Tyson.

"The Manhattanhenge" is the combination of forces of man and nature, which produces a momentary sight so spectacular that one has to stop everything, and in sheer amazement, marvel at its awesome beauty.

It is when the man-made city buildings are perfectly symmetrical on both sides of nature's gorgeous sun as it sets in such a perfect position down the center of a New York City street.

People from many miles away come to view this magnificent sight.

It lasts for just a few seconds.

For those few seconds, it seems like man and the universe are in perfect harmony.

Witnesses to this event feel like they are connected majestically to the voice and powers of the universe.

They feel as if everything in the world is exactly where it should be - that the universe is in perfect balance and in symmetry.

That the pieces all fit together.

That there really is a universal plan, a plan that goes unnoticed but for a few seconds, twice a year.

After viewing the Manhattanhenge, it is only natural for people to then take the time and reflect on their own life and its majesty.

I believe it is during reflection, after witnessing nature's beauty, that we get the operating instructions of life.

Louis Schwartzberg said:

"Nature slows you down to appreciate the moment by connecting what is the deeper part of your soul.

You appreciate the little things in life.

It cultivates gratitude.

It cultivates compassion. "

For some time now I have had a date set with my youngest daughter Cassidy to go view this year's Manhattanhenge.

The day came and went.

We did not go.

Something in her life suddenly came up.

More resistance.

There are so many things that I want to do in life, and I don't.

There are so many places I want to go in life, and I haven't.

There are so many things I want to say to people who are hurting - and I remain silent.

I have allowed the resistance of every day life to get in my way.

I have had enough tragedy in my life to understand the importance of doing, seeing and saying all that I know I should.

But I haven't.

To make more good than bad come from my daughter's situation.

That is the goal.

To be the pebble.

I know I needed to see the Manhattanhenge.

But I didn't.

Resistance was stronger than my will.

I need to change that.

- 6 -
NATURE KNOCKING

You don't hear
What is truly important in life
With your ears.
You hear it with your heart.

The universe works in mysterious ways.

It is determined to have me solve its clues.

It is 5:30 a.m. on a Monday morning in June.

School is in the rear view mirror and summer is on the horizon.

I am driving east on Sunrise Highway on Long Island.

A highway that is so appropriately named.

The sunrise is spectacular.

The suns rays are blinding.

The sun is rising up the center of the road on the horizon.

The trees are perfectly symmetrical on both sides of the rising sun.

It is my own personal Manhattanhenge.

It is as if the universe is saying to me, "If you keep canceling on us, we are just going to have to come to you."

I take in the magnificence of the scene.

Its initial effects on me are minimized due to my mood.

More resistance.

To say that I am less than ecstatic about driving my son Maverick to work this early in the morning is an understatement.

I do though, as it is my solution to the problem of having two vehicles in my household and four people needing to use them.

Day after day for the last few weeks I have been reluctantly making this same trip and never once making the connection between the coincidences in my life, and the beauty of nature staring me right in the eye.

The game of charades is currently in progress in my life.

My subconscious mind is using nature and its beauty to give me clues.

The beach ball is rising near the surface again.

I suddenly have this overwhelming feeling of truly knowing.

Nature has aligned its beauty and magnificence to bring memories of Bill to the forefront of my mind.

There has only been one other time in my life when I drove to work traveling east into a sunrise.

Some thirty-one years ago when Bill was my boss.

I remind myself of this coincidence.

I believe this coincidence is a clue.

I believe the reason I needed to drive Maverick to work this early in the morning was to experience my own personal "Manhattanhenge".

I take a few seconds in stillness and I combine the coincidence with the beauty of nature.

They say that suffering and beauty often appear together in life.

A thought comes rushing up through my gut.

What if what I want to say to Bill - and don't, could be exactly what he needed to hear - and didn't?

You go through life and you never tell people how much you care about them.

We probably should all do that more often.

- 7 -
Care Is There

It is beautiful to express love
And even more beautiful to feel it.

Dejan Stojanovic

For me, the hardest part of being a caregiver is the seclusion I feel from the world.

It is a feeling that the world I was once a part of is being lived without me in it.

I have this contradictory desire to be in two different places at the same time - to be part of the world and to take care of a loved one.

Rationally, I understand fulfilling both desires is not simultaneously possible.

If I were only able to live one life, I undoubtedly would choose to live the life secluded from the world, taking care of Jess.

And I have no problem with that.

I would make that same choice, without any qualms, 100% of the time.

What makes my choice easier to execute is when the world stops for a moment and lets me know it understands why I am not there, that I am still an important part of it and that I am missed.

My day started today with a phone call from an old friend, one whom I haven't spoken to in a few years.

During our conversation he says to me,

"John, I just want you to know we haven't spoken in a while – but I think about and pray for you and your family everyday."

Hearing those simple sincere words gave me such a good feeling.

A feeling that lasted the whole afternoon.

Later that evening, I received a private message from a Facebook friend whom I haven't seen since high school.

It read,

"John, I was just wondering how Jess was?
I just want you to know I think of you and your family all the time.

I pray for you constantly.

I wish you all the best."

Timing is everything in life.

As today was the six-year anniversary of Jess losing oxygen to her brain.

Neither of my two friends had any way of knowing.

I know it is not a coincidence that the universe made them communicate their care for me, at the exact time I needed to feel it.

Anne Frank wrote: "How wonderful it is that nobody need wait a single moment before starting to improve this world."

With just a few heartfelt words, two people made a vast difference in my day.

In the way I felt.

In my outlook.

In my ability to get through a trying day.

The universe surely works in mysterious ways.

The power of caring words.

They are great to hear.

I am so grateful my two friends were kind enough to transfer their thoughts from inside their heads to my heart.

As Oscar Wilde said, "The smallest act of kindness is worth more than the grandest intention."

I know now I must do the same.

I need to let Bill know that I am thinking of him.

And his family.

Before today, my sharing that complicatedly simple message with Bill didn't seem like I was doing enough.

Now I know that it is.

- 8 -
TRULY KNOWING

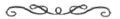

I'm doing what I know how to do,
As well as I know how to do it.

Stephen King
On Writing: The Memoir of the Craft

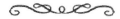

It is the combination of experiencing my own Manhattanhenge and the kind words I received from my two friends that convinces me my game of charades is over.

I have solved my subconscious mind's clue.

Henry David Thoreau said: "If you can speak what you never hear, if you can write what you never read, you have done rare things."

I must do rare things.

I must use the circumstances of my life as a catalyst to spread kindness by expressing my feelings to the people who have made a difference in my life.

There is a saying – Namaste' which means "the divine in me recognizes the divine in you."

I need to connect the divine.

The best way I know how.

I must write.

I must write to Bill and express to him what I should have expressed to him years ago.

That he is a good man.

That although he is presently secluded from the world, he is cared about and missed.

And I hope, beyond almost anything I have ever hoped for, that somehow by my doing so will give Bill a good feeling.

That will last his whole day.

Which will improve his outlook.

And help him get through a trying time.

As Mahatma Gandhi said:

"Action expresses priorities."

I must do so today.

PART II

One repays a teacher badly
If one remains nothing but a pupil.

Friedrich Nietzsche

- 9 -
A VALUABLE NICKEL

There's no way to know
What makes one thing happen
Or not happen.
What leads to what.
What destroys what.
What causes what
To flourish or die
Or take another course.

Cheryl Strayed
Wild

The year was 1983.

I was a senior in high school.

My dad had been out of work for the better part of the prior two years.

The technological revolution had just started to hit the printing industry.

It hit it hard.

We felt it.

To say my family didn't have any discretionary income at the time was being kind.

I remember there was an awards dinner after my wrestling season.

My final wrestling season.

I was scheduled to get an award.

I didn't go.

It cost $10 to attend - $10 that my family didn't have.

I decided not to let my mother know about the awards dinner because I knew that she would have somehow come up with the $10.

And I also knew she could have used that $10 for something else.

It was more important for me not to put any more financial pressure on my mom than it was for me to receive the award.

So I never told her about it.

I just didn't go.

Also in 1983, New York State just passed a new law – the bottle return deposit law.

Going forward, all bottles would have a nickel deposit.

This deposit would be paid by the consumer at the time of purchase and would be refunded to them when they returned the empty bottles to the store.

At the time, I had no idea how impactful this new law would be on my life.

My Junior High wrestling coach, Mr. Hurley, had a brother who had just opened up a beverage store.

This new law was adversely affecting his business.

He needed to hire someone.

I needed a job.

My coach brokered the deal.

"John, how would you like a job for the summer?

It's nothing earth shattering, but you would be able to get as many hours as you like, and you would be working with good people.

Plus, you get to work in the Hamptons for the summer.

And by the way, the good person I am talking about is my brother, Bill."

As a teenager, the only thing I heard from my coach's offer was, "The Hamptons for the summer."

The "You'll be working with good people" part had no influence on my taking the job.

But it would be the part that would have the greatest influence on my life.

- 10 -
My Boss

As I would not be a slave,
So I would not be a master.

Abraham Lincoln

It is funny what the mind remembers.

I am an avid baseball fan, yet if you were to ask me which team lost in the 2011 World Series; I would stare at you blankly as I searched my mind for the answer.

I love food, yet if you were to ask me what I had for lunch a year ago, I wouldn't be able to tell you with any confidence.

If you were to ask me to tell you the color of the pants I am wearing today, without looking - I couldn't.

The reason is that none of these things or events has had any impact on my life.

Working with Billy did.

That is probably why I vividly remember my first day on the job.

The one on which I showed up two hours late.

"The Hamptons" wound up being East Hampton.

The furthest Hampton town from my home.

The Hamptons are located from my home in this order and distance: Westhampton (10 miles), Hampton Bays (16 miles), Southampton (22 miles), Bridgehampton (42 miles) and then East Hampton (60 miles).

East Hampton - 60 miles away.

Add in summer traffic.

Add in the fact that there is only one lane entering the town.

Hence, my tardiness.

I remember pulling up to Peconic Beverage two hours late for my first day at work, bracing myself to be balled out by my new boss.

Instead, I was met with a laugh, a smile and a solution.

"I'm here to work for you," I said as I entered the store.

Bill smiled and said, "I kind of expected you'd be late. Summer traffic in the Hamptons is murder."

"I didn't realize how far this was. It's actually 60 miles from my house," I said.

Knowing me for less than 60 seconds Bill said:

"You come highly recommended by my brother.

He tells me you're a good person.

Here is what I'm going to do.

I'm going to pay for your gas, arrange your hours to minimize your time in traffic and increase the hours you work each day so you will be able to get the same hours but make one less trip a week.

This will all help to keep you sane."

He hesitated for a second and then he said,

"And by the way, you don't work for me – you work with me.

There is a huge difference."

Yes, there is.

Making someone feel like they are an equal, and part of something bigger than themselves is the greatest asset a parent, a boss or any leader can have.

It brings out the best in people.

I am not saying that there is no hierarchy in life in certain situations; we all know there is.

What I am saying is - the people who make others feel like there is no hierarchy are the ones who will get the most out of another person.

Great people make other people feel great.

Looking back on my life, I find it pretty ironic that the only person I ever referred to as "my boss", never once bossed me around.

In these non-hierarchal environments, instead of looking up or down, people look within.

And it is within where greatness resides.

Imagine if we all treated each other as equals.

What a concept.

What if that simple thought was carried out in real life?

There would be no racism.

No sexism.

No genocide.

No class structure.

No Ferguson, Missouri.

No glass ceilings.

I guess John Lennon was on to something.

Bill had the chance to instill his hierarchy on me on my
first day on the job – and he didn't.
Instead, he gave me the feeling of being an equal.

A feeling I never forgot.

- 11 -
LEAD BY EXAMPLE

A man who wants to lead the orchestra
must turn his back on the crowd.

Max Lucado

For the better part of my first day on the job, Bill showed me around the store and explained to me what I would be doing during my "summer in the Hamptons."

I had a two-pronged job description - I was to take care of the customers at the register and sort "empties" in the back of the building.

I would go back and forth, depending on which area needed my help the most.

Working the cash register was the fun and easy part.

Sorting empties was not.

On my first day, I worked by Bill's side.

At one point in the day, Bill felt comfortable enough to leave me to work with the other store workers as he attended to other matters.

After he left, there was a slow but constant flow of customers in the store, which with the help of the other workers I was able to handle with no problems.

A good hour went by and I hadn't seen Bill.

When a break in the customer flow occurred, I headed to find the bathroom.

While on my way to the bathroom I looked for Bill.

He was nowhere to be found.

My initial reaction was, "This guy is going to be one of those bosses who makes you do all the work while he does nothing in an office somewhere."

I walked past his office on my way to the bathroom.

It was empty.

I finally made it to the bathroom, which was down a very narrow hallway; cases of soda and beer were stacked on each side.

I scurried down the narrow hallway to the bathroom door.

The door was ajar so I figured the bathroom was empty.

As I opened the door I realized I was wrong.

I walked in on Bill - in the bathroom.

More accurately...

I walked in on Bill on his hands and knees in the bathroom.

Cleaning the floor.

"What the heck are you doing?" I asked.

"I'm cleaning the bathroom," Bill said.

My initial reaction blurted unfiltered out of my mouth,

"Why are you cleaning the bathroom?
I mean aren't you the boss - can't you just make someone else do that?"

I will never forget his response.

He said, "How can I ever ask someone to do something I am unwilling to do myself?"

It has been often said that Steve Jobs changed the world.

Sometimes I think - not always for the better.

At least for parents.

There is no doubt that Steve Job's passion to create a device that could store all of a person's music in the palm of one's hand revolutionized the world.

But it also came with some unintended consequences for parents.

For the first time in history, parents were no longer part of their kid's music purchases.

All of a sudden, every kid had the freedom to acquire and listen to "their" music without his or her parents being able to listen in.

In the old days, if a kid was blasting music with questionable lyrics, a parent was able to hear it and make the necessary adjustments.

After Steve Jobs invented the iPod that was no longer possible.

Old school skills of music censoring by parents became obsolete.

New skills were needed.

Hence the surprise iPod check.

My attempt at filtering which songs were right for my kids to listen to has been the cause of many a fight in my house over the years.

One day after doing a surprise inspection of my son's iPod, I was livid.

I demanded he delete all the songs on his iPod which had lyrics alluding to sex, drugs, violence or profanity.

This would have basically cleaned out his whole newly acquired song catalogue on his iPod.

We argued.

The basis of his argument was that I was a being a hypocrite. He felt that many of the songs on my iPod referred to similar subject matters.

I laughed.

I said, "You won't find a single song on my iPod that even remotely comes close to having questionable song lyrics like yours do."

He immediately grabbed my iPod, spun the click wheel to "Bohemian Rhapsody" and pressed play.

"Mama, I just killed a man.

I put a gun against his head

Pulled my trigger now he's dead."

"Do you really think I am going to go out and kill a man after listening to this song?" I said trying to pull the words back into my mouth as soon as I said them.

"Mama Mia, mama Mia", I heard the song continue.

"Easy come, easy go...will you let me go?" The song played on.

I had a choice to make.

I could either delete Bohemian Rhapsody from my iPod or prove to my son that I was asking him to do something I was unwilling to do myself.

"How can I ever ask someone to do something I am unwilling to do myself?"

"I will not let you go," the song played on.

Oh, yes I will.

And I did.

I don't believe that listening to Bohemian Rhapsody has ever made me want to kill a man, but from that day to this, you will not find that song on my iPhone.

How could I possibly have one set of rules for myself and another set for my kids?

- 12 -
THE COST OF AN ENEMY

'Tis best to weigh the enemy
More mighty than he seems.

William Shakespeare

There were two kinds of customers who brought back empties to the store.

The first kind was the customer who washed out each bottle or can before bringing them back.

These customers were also the ones who neatly stacked each can in a case tray, making it quick and easy to get an accurate count.

The transaction was clean, quick and accurate.

This type of customer was a pleasure to serve.

The second type of customer was the one who returned unwashed cans in a garbage bag.

A garbage bag that had been sealed and left to ferment in the summer sun.
We called this the "empty juice."

When a customer brought their empties back this way, I was trained to politely remind them that it was the store's policy for the customer to place each can in a case tray so we could get an accurate count.

Either one of two things happened with this type of customer.

Either they took the empties out of the bag when they were reminded to do so, or they didn't.

If they didn't, and there were other customers waiting, they would have to wait until all the other customers were helped before we reached into their bag and pulled each can out for them.

With every reach into the garbage bag, the "empty juice", would get all over your hands and arms.

This second customer type was to be avoided at all costs.

They were not fun to wait on.

There were many celebrities that came into the East Hampton store during the summer.

On any normal, day it wouldn't be surprising to see Dudley Moore, Ralph Lauren or Billy Joel trying to blend in as normal folk.

As hard as they tried to act like locals, you still knew who they were.

One day there was one celebrity who blended in as a local all too well.

As customer type #2.

This unrecognized celebrity threw his garbage bag full of empties up on the counter and looked at me, waiting for me to take each can out of the bag for him.

I reminded him of the stores policy that in order to make the transaction as fast and accurate as possible it would be helpful if he placed each can in a case tray.

He stared at me.

A blank stare, sort of a Frankenstein - looking stare.

He muttered something inaudible.

I went on to help the rest of the other customers who had properly placed their empties in case trays.

After helping all the other customers, I realized this mans empties were still in his bag.

He was waiting for me to reach into the bag and get each empty out.

Which I did.

"Empty juice" galore dripped all over my arms.

After I completed my count of his empties, I handed him a receipt for $2.70 for the 54 cans he had returned.

He looked at the receipt and said,

"I had 55 cans.

This should be for $2.75."

I stared at him.

He stared back at me.

Being that he didn't put each can in a case tray to be accurately counted, I bypassed this step and kept count in my head.

Maybe I made a mistake.

That was quite possible.

No problem. I would just correct the receipt to reflect 55 cans returned and the problem would be solved, I thought to myself.

Then it dawned on me. This guy did the same thing to me last week, and the week before that.

He was the *"You shorted me a nickel"* guy.

I corrected "my mistake."

I handed him a new receipt for $2.75.

But with this new realization, I also reached into my pocket, took out a quarter and said,

"Let's save some time. Take this quarter as upfront payment for the next five times you come in."

He stared through me this time, his veins bulging on both sides of his neck.

He took the updated receipt and the quarter from me and headed to the front of the store to find the owner to complain to about me.

"Are you the owner?" He said waving the quarter in the air.

"Yes - I'm Billy."

"Holy crap, Billy! That boy back there tried to cheat me. He shorted me a nickel."
"You mean John?" Bill said pointing in my direction.

"Yea, that one back there."

"Is everything straightened out?"

"Yea, but he tries to cheat me every time I come in here."

"Nah, I find that hard to believe. John is one of my best workers. If he made a mistake I guarantee it was an honest one."

"You should do something about him."

"The only thing I'm going to do with John is give him a raise," Bill said downplaying the event as best he could.

It was only later in the day when Bill and I spoke about the situation, I learned the *"You shorted me a nickel"* guy was a movie star.

He starred in some monster movie in the '70's.

After learning the identity of the *"You shorted me a nickel"* guy I said, "I don't care who he is, he comes in every week and does the same thing. He's wrong."

Bill said to me,

"You're right. He is wrong.

But you probably should have kept the quarter in your pocket."

It took me a real long time to learn "to keep the quarter in my pocket."

So many times that quarter has gotten me into trouble. The problem may have already been solved moments earlier, but before I can let it go, I have to get my jab in.

That jab turns into a counter punch and all of a sudden it's a fight.

An enemy is made.

Knowing how to solve a confrontation without escalating it is a gift.

When I learned to leave that quarter in my pocket, unnecessary enemies were averted.

When I learned to add kindness to a confrontation, I realized that instead of making an enemy, I could gain an ally.

"I'm sorry sir.

55 cans it is.

Here is a new receipt for $2.75.

Have a great day."

It is not worth making an enemy over a nickel.

Even if you are right.

It is better to kill your enemies with kindness.

They hate that.

- 13 -
Ask, Listen, Implement

The greatest compliment ever paid to me
Was when one asked me what I thought
And attended to my answer.

Henry David Thoreau

It couldn't have been more than a few months after I started working at Peconic Beverage when Bill began to ask my opinion on matters in the store.

"What product do you think we should display here?" he would ask.

"Why?" And he would give me time to back up my answer.

"You know – that makes sense, I'm going to go with that."

And he would.

Just like that.

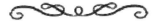

Valuing someone else's opinion seems like such a small deal.

It is not.

It is one of the greatest compliments one person can pay to another.

To ask what one thinks, or how one feels is being considerate.

To truly listen, understand and implement what one thinks is the greatest compliment you can give a person.

You are sending a message that their voice is important.

Everyone wants to feel important.

Soren Kierkegaard said:

"Presence is infinitely more rewarding than productivity."

- 14 -
Little Things

Practice yourself
For heaven's sake
In little things
Then proceed to greater.

Epictetus

Over the course of the next few months working at Peconic Beverage I started noticing some things.

Little things.

For instance, when a customer entered the store with properly sorted empties, cleaned and in trays, Bill would hesitate to act, which would allow me to wait on that customer.

And when a customer came into the store carrying a trash bag full of empties seeping with empty juice, Bill would be the first one to wait on them.

Or when Shaky Ray came in at exactly 12:02 pm everyday for his six-pack of Black Label, he would somehow wait in line until Bill was able to wait on him.

When Bill was available, Shaky Ray would put his six-pack on the counter, he would extend and open his hand which was full of coin.

The coins would shake more than dishes in a closet during an earthquake.

Bill would patiently and compassionately reach into the palm of his hand and take out exactly $2.33 in change.

Shaky Ray would say, "You got it?"

And Bill would say, "I got it. Thank you."

That exchange would happen every day.

I also noticed when a popular item suddenly went on sale, it wasn't because it was close to being out of date or that we were trying to get rid of its inventory.

It was because Bill negotiated a better price from the manufacturer and decided to pass along the savings to the customer.

Savings that quite easily could have gone to his bottom line but instead were shared with the customer.

Little things.

But I noticed.

People always do.

There have been a few times in my life when I was so focused on accomplishing a big thing that I overlooked little things, feeling they were not as important.

I have since learned that they are what is important.

No big thing ever gets accomplished unless the little things are true.

No business gets built unless you genuinely care about people.

No life improves unless you value and appreciate each day.

Big things are just a compilation of a whole lot of little things.

Big things are hard to accomplish.

Little things are not.

No matter what our circumstances may be, we all have the ability to accomplish little things every day.

And before you know it, BIG things happen.

- 15 -
WHEN A STATION WAGON IS MORE VALUABLE THAN A RED FERRARI

I have learned
To be with those I love
Is enough.

Walt Whitman

East Hampton is a beach town.

In the summer the store would be filled with people in bathing suits.

One day, two twenty-something year old girls in bikini's came into the store and started flirting with Bill.

Just like Christie Brinkley did in "National Lampoon's Vacation" when she pulled her red Ferrari along side Clarke Griswold's station wagon and flirted with him as his wife slept in the passenger seat.

It was all very innocent.

Until it wasn't.

Just as suddenly as Christie Brinkley stripped and jumped into the pool to skinny-dip and urged Clarke to join her – the two girls in bikini's did the same.

The two girls in the bikinis didn't actually strip and go skinny-dipping, but they might as well have.

Their flirting quickly escalated to an offer.

I remember very clearly what Bill said as he twirled his wedding ring on his finger.

"I'm flattered – but I'm married."

But it was in the way he said, "I'm married."

It wasn't "I'm married – are you OK with that?"

It was "I'm married" - STOP SIGN.

The two girls didn't pick up on the difference.

They said, "We're fine with that."

In which Bill replied, "I'm sorry – I'm not."

At the time the eighteen-year-old version of myself thought Bill was crazy.

Today the fifty-year-old version of myself understands he was brilliant.

Character is doing the right thing, which is always the hard thing, even when no one is watching.

Too many people think the right thing is doing what you want to do, regardless of how it would affect others, and the wrong thing is only to get caught.

Not many people in this world understand when a station wagon is more valuable than the red Ferrari.

- 16 -
MR. MONEYBAGS

My father gave me the greatest gift
Anyone could give another person.
He believed in me.

Jim Valvano

One of my responsibilities when I closed the store at night was to make a bank deposit.

After locking the store, I would count the cash in the register, put it in a bank bag and drop it off at the bank down the road.

The drop off took place after 11 pm, while the bank was closed for business, so I would drop it down a special chute designed for night deposits for businesses.

Every night I would open the chute, drop in the bag, close the chute and then reopen it to make sure the bag dropped down into the bank's vault.

One night when I was making the deposit, I opened the chute, I put the moneybag in the chute and I closed it.

I then reopened the chute to make sure the bag fell down into the vault.

It did not.

There was something stuck in the chute obstructing it from going down.

I reached in to find out what it was.

I pushed and pulled on the item – it was really stuck.

With one big yank the item came flying out of the chute.

It stayed in my grasp.

There I was, a poor eighteen-year-old kid, in the dark, with no one around for miles, in an age before video cameras and cell phones, holding a bag full of untraceable money.

The last person to make a night deposit forgot to reopen the chute to make sure their money went down correctly, and their moneybag got stuck in the chute.

I had a decision to make.

Do I quickly open the chute and push the bag of money back down or do I just take the bag of money and go home like nothing had happened?

If I took the bag of money, no one would ever know.

There would be no way to trace the missing money back to me.

One side of my brain rationalized that it wasn't like I set out to steal a bag full of money, it just happened to be there - sort of a lucky find on my part.

When I got to work the next morning I asked Bill if I could speak with him in private, as I had a confession to make.

I told Bill about the moneybag I had found in the chute the night before.

I let him know that I was positive that nobody saw me.

And I stopped my story right there.

I led him believe I took the bag.

I studied his body language and facial expression looking for a hint of what to say next.

It then dawned on me.

Bill wasn't hoping that I did the right thing.

He *knew* I did the right thing.

Never once did he ever falter in his belief that I would do the right thing, even in the midst of unforeseen temptation.

That was a great feeling.

I finally confessed that I pushed the moneybag back into the chute so fast that it made my head spin.

I'll never forget what he said to me when I voiced an almost remorseful thought about doing the right thing,

"Nobody would ever have known..." I said.

He said,

"You are right. Nobody would ever have known.

That is.

Nobody - except for you."

To thine own self be true, and it must follow, as the night the day, thou canst not then be false to any man.

William Shakespeare

- 17 -
LET'S NOT GO TO THE VIDEOTAPE

The best way to find out
If you can trust somebody
Is to trust them.

Ernest Hemingway

Sometimes after cashing out the register during the day, the amount of money that was in the draw wouldn't match the amount the register said should be in the draw.

When this occurred Bill would be in his office for hours trying to figure out what had happened.

Was there a voided transaction that caused the error?

Why were there so many voided transactions?

Was someone stealing money from the register?

I'm sure these were all questions that went through his mind as he tried to figure out where and why the deficit occurred.

On one such day, after Bill spent hours trying to figure this out, I asked him a question.

"Bill, why don't you just install a video camera in the store and point it at the cash register?"

His reply was classic Bill.

He said, "I'll never have a video camera in the store. I don't want my employees feeling like I don't trust them. That doesn't make for a good work environment."

He went on to say, "I have to believe the people who work with me will do the right thing even when no one is watching. I know installing a camera would help, but that's not the environment I want to manage in."

It is better to trust someone and have them violate that trust than it is to live in a world without trust.

It is better to love someone and have your heart broken than it is to have never experienced love.
It is better to believe in someone and have them disappoint you than it is to live in a world without belief.

To trust, to love and to believe is opening oneself to being vulnerable.

There will be times when you are burned by doing so.

Trust, believe and love anyway.

Overall, the world is a much better place when you do.

- 18 -
SPONTANEOUS COMBUSTION

Pleasure in the job
Puts perfection in the work.

Aristotle

My "summer in the Hamptons" was winding down.

It was the dog days of August.

The days were long, hot and chaotic.

During one of these dog days I was working the cash register and Bill was out on a delivery.

The flow in the store was constant, the pace was fierce.

Out of nowhere I heard a loud BOOM.

An explosion.

The stifling hot warehouse increased the carbonation pressure of a 2-liter soda and made it explode.
Just like that.

This spontaneous combustion wasn't a totally new phenomenon to me.

A few hours before, when I was walking by a pallet of soda in the warehouse, a spontaneous combustion of a 2-liter bottle initiated me with my first "soda shower".

I don't know if the long summer tired me out, or if I was just in a mischievous mood on the day of the BOOM, but the explosion triggered something in my head.

I asked myself, "What if these spectacular spontaneous combustions could be induced at will?"

Later in the day, after the customer flow had died down, I went out back to prove my thesis.

I rationalized that I was doing research, sort of a science experiment for the good of mankind.

I took a few 2-liter soda bottles out of warehouse inventory and I went outside to the employee parking lot which was a large open space in the back of the store.

A perfect environment for my experiment.

I can remember taking a 2-liter soda bottle and shaking it for thirty seconds to really increase the pressure inside the bottle and then....

I bent at the knees and I heaved the bottle straight up in the air.

I remember the ten or so seconds that the bottle was in an upward trajectory, and during that time, the experiment seemed like a great idea.

But as soon as the bottle reached its zenith and started plummeting downward with momentum I had a change of heart.

I wanted to take back my actions.

It was too late.

There was no stopping the forces now.

The perfect soda storm had been created.

With the combined elements of the increased pressure of the carbonated soda, the heat, the flight and the force of gravity, I had formed an instant soda rocket.

The bottle hit the ground with such great force.

That as soon as it touched the ground, the bottle reversed course and instantly flew off like a missile towards the back entrance of the parking lot.

At the exact same time Bill was returning from his delivery.

The highly pressurized flying soda bottle just missed hitting Bill's truck when he entered the parking lot.

I will never forget what happened next.

Bill got out of his truck, walked over to me and said,

"Let's see what happens if we take this piece of plastic off of the bottom of the bottle. It's probably just acting as extra weight."

And we did.

It actually perfected the trajectory of the bottle during flight.

For the next forty-five minutes Bill and I launched "Soda Rockets".

We launched "Soda Rockets" over the roof of the restaurant next door, into the back brush; we launched them for height and we launched them for accuracy.

We launched them to let off some steam from working so hard.

We launched them to celebrate the end of the summer.

To this day I remember Bill being the last one in the parking lot launching "Soda Rockets" as I went back to work.

With a renewed sense of enthusiasm.

Because when work is fun, it is not considered work at all.

- 19 -
SUMMER BONUS

Our brightest blazes of gladness
Are commonly kindled
By unexpected sparks.

Samuel Johnson

When the summer drew to a close, I presumed my job did too. I understood I had only been hired for the summer season.

I was handed an envelope.

Inside the envelope was a check for two weeks pay.

With a note attached saying to enjoy my summer bonus.

"What is this Bill?"

> "It's your summer bonus. We give two bonuses' each year. One at the end of the summer and you will be getting your other one around Thanksgiving."

"What do you mean 'my other one'? I said.

I thought this job was just for the summer - that the winters were absolutely dead?"

"You always stick with good people during hard times. Good people are hard to find. When you find one, you do everything you can to hold onto them."

I once worked for a multi-billion-dollar corporation that wondered why their work force had such low morale.

This was the same corporation which scheduled their employees for only 19 hours for the week. Strategically and carefully staying under 20 hours a week which would have qualified them for health care benefits.

This was the same corporation whose CEO voted to give himself a $2-million-dollar year end bonus while giving his employees a choice between a Boars Head turkey or Boars Head ham for their holiday bonus.

It's not that I was ungrateful for the ham or turkey.

But I would think the idea of giving a bonus is to make one feel like they are part of something, not like there is a moat separating you from the company.

This company's way of improving morale was to get rid of the employees with the "bad attitudes" and hire new employees.

Over time I finally realized the company's true intention wasn't to hire new employees with better attitudes, it was to look for new employees that had a much longer spoiling time.

They continued their shenanigans with their new employees.

Miraculously, right around holiday bonus time of the following year, the company realized they had hired workers who had just as bad an attitude as the previous ones.

Hmmm.

When you take care of people, they know it.

They become loyal.

They will do anything for you.

When you find a good person in your life – stick with them.

Through the winters and the hard times.

Spring comes before you know it.

One day it's summer again.

Seasons change.

Good people seldom do.

They remain good people.

And there is nobody better to go through a winter with than a good person.

- 20 -
WINTER DARKNESS

The flower that blooms in adversity,
Is the rarest and most beautiful of all.

Mulan

The winters at Peconic Beverage were cold, dark and desolate.

In reality it would have taken only one person to run the store - business was that slow.

Bill kept four of us on board that winter.

In the summertime the pace was utter chaotic, always running from one customer to the next.
The store was always filled and there was a constant flow of customer traffic.

In the winter the store was still, and most of the time hours passed between customers.

The flow was slow. When more than one customer was in the store at the same time, it was considered a winter rush.

Having four people employed at this time was totally unnecessary.

Bill did it to take care of those he considered "good people".

Hard times are hard.

Twice as hard as you ever thought they would be.

They last twice as long as you ever expect them to.

Winters are dark.

Darker than you could ever imagine.

There is nothing that helps get you through dark times better than good people.

- 21 -
WHOLE SEASONS

Human greatness
Does not lie in wealth or power,
But in character and goodness.

Anne Frank

In John Mackey's book "Conscious Capitalism" he tells the story of when Whole Foods was just starting out.

Early in the company's history, when Whole Foods had only four stores, Texas was hit with a great flood.

It wiped Whole Foods out.

They lost everything.

All inventory.

All equipment.

All hope.

All four of its stores were completely flooded.

Absolute and utter destruction.

They had no resources to recover.

They had no cash, no credit and no way of rebuilding.

In his book, John Mackey reminisces about the day after the rains had stopped when he literally swam to one of the Whole Foods stores.

When he arrived after the mile swim he was surprised by what he saw.

Total strangers were uniting to rebuild the Whole Foods store.

Strangers had cleaned up the debris, they pumped out the water, they swept away the dirt.

They offered him money.

Vendors extended him credit.

The store recovered.

When John Mackey asked the strangers why they did what they did without being asked they replied,

"We love and believe in Whole Foods.
It is a good thing and you are a good man.

We just couldn't see it destroyed.

We just had to help rebuild it.

It means that much to us."

Whole Foods currently has 2,100 locations and produces over $11 Billion dollars in annual revenue.

It has been the primary catalyst for healthier eating in millions of our lives.

And in the process, it has touched the lives of millions of people in a positive way.

It is amazing what Whole Foods has turned into.

To think if it weren't for the kindness of total strangers, Whole Foods wouldn't exist today.

I have lived through a few Hurricanes during my life.

The only one I can ever remember wanting to clean up after was "Hurricane Gloria" in 1985.

I have a keen recollection of how important it was for me to help Peconic Beverage reopen after the storm.

I remember driving around debris, fallen trees and downed power poles.

Somehow I traveled the 60 miles and I helped in the clean up, working beside Bill, other employees and store customers.

Why did we all do this?

Because we loved Peconic Beverage and Bill was a good man.

I figured Bill was willing to stick with me during the winter, the least I could do in return was to be there for him during the storm.

We all need love, especially in our time of need.

A company with 11 billion dollars in annual sales would have failed to exist if it didn't get love at the right time.

Imagine, a few people's love allowed Whole Foods to go from 4 stores to 2,100 stores and 11 billion in sales.

Every one of us has an opportunity to do the same thing.

We all see people in need every day of our lives.

Dante wrote: "He who sees a need and waits to be asked for help is as unkind as if he refused it."

Act before being asked.

We each can be there for one another, providing hope and kindness in the midst of utter devastation.

Not allowing a good person or a good thing to die.

To rebuild.

To keep the mission alive.

Imagine if this rebuilding concept is duplicated 278 million times daily in the United States.

Imagine how many "Whole Lives" we could rebuild.

It has been said the way you value a life lived is by the army that comes together in its time of need.

If you value ones' life, be there to help rebuild that life after a storm has hits.

Everyone alive today has a teetering Whole Foods in their lives they could help resurrect.

Imagine the difference you will make by showing up, without being asked, when all hope seems to be lost.

2,100 stores and 11 billion in revenue magnified 278 million times.

Imagine.

- 22 -
Grand Theft Auto

Money is the best bait to fish for men.

Thomas Fuller

My car was leaking oil.

I debated about letting the buyer know.

I wanted $2,000 for the car so I figured I would start my asking price at $2,500, knowing that after learning about the oil leak the buyer would try and chew me down.

"$2,500 – not a problem," the potential buyer said.

"You're asking $2,500, but I'll give you $3,000 if you leave your license plates on the car for a few days until I can register it. I'll be back tomorrow with the money."

Bill overheard some of the conversation I had with the potential buyer and he asked me, "Did you sell your car?"

After telling him about the extra $500 I unexpectedly made he said,

"I'm glad for you but something is not quite right.

You told him about the oil leak and instead of trying to chew you down in price he offered you $500 more?

Don't take it. Only take the $2,500.

You really wanted $2,000, so you got an extra $500 already."

"Yea, but now I can get an extra $1,000," I said.

"Don't be greedy. Trust me, something is fishy," Bill said.

I asked him if he knew the buyers.

He did, and he didn't give them a glowing endorsement.

"Make sure you get cash."

The next day the two guys came back.

I informed them that I'd take the $2,500 instead of the $3,000 for the car.

"Are you sure about that? You're leaving an easy $500 on the table. It's just for a day," they asked.

"I'm sure," I said.

But I actually wasn't sure.

I definitely could have used the extra $500 and I didn't see how it could come back to hurt me by taking it.

The bait looked so appetizing,

It always does when you don't see the hook.

I guess that's the art of baiting a hook – to show the bait and to hide the hook.

How ever tempting the extra $500 seemed, Bill convinced me not to bite at the bait.

I reluctantly listened.

I completed the transaction making $500 less than I could have.

A few days went by.

I was sorting empties in the back of the store when I saw two gentlemen in suits approach Bill in the front of the store.

They talked for a few seconds and then Bill pointed towards me.

The two gentlemen in suits then started to move quickly toward me as if they expected me to run out the back of the store.

I didn't.

I stood there frozen.

When the two guys in the suits realized I wasn't going to run, they slowed down their pace.

"Are you John Passaro?" one detective asked.

"Yes - I – am, why?" I asked slowly.

"Do you own a 1976 Mustang?"

"I did."

"What do you mean you did?" The other detective said.

"I sold it last week. Two guys came in and bought it on the spot."

The officers weren't convinced, until I added,

"They offered me an extra $500 to leave the plates on the car for a few days, until they could register it. But I didn't take it."

"That was the smartest thing you will ever do in your life, son." The good detective said.

"What do you mean?" I asked.

"That car was used to hold up an OTB in Southampton last night.

Two masked men with assault rifles.

If you had left those plates on the car you would be coming with us.

For a long time."

- 23 -
NEW COKE

The distance between insanity and genius
Lies only in success.

Bruce Feirstein

In the 1980's Coca-Cola's lead over Pepsi had been slowly and steadily slipping for quite some time.

In 1985 Coca-Cola decided to change the 99-year-old formula of Coke in hopes of recapturing its lost consumers.

This was a big event in the world at the time.

This new version of Coke was introduced with no shortage of hype and fanfare.

On April 23rd, 1985 Coca-Cola announced they would no longer be making any more of the original formula version of Coca-Cola, they would only be making New Coke going forward.

With high anticipation, people awaited the arrival of this New Coke.

As would anyone who owned a beverage center, Bill stocked up on New Coke.

He bought pallets and pallets of it.

He tied up money for New Coke, money that should have gone elsewhere, feeling that the turnover in the inventory of New Coke would be quick and he would then be able to use that money and more for its intended purposes.

The highly anticipated day finally came.

New Coke arrived.

And people hated it.

That may be putting it to lightly.

People loathed the taste of New Coke.

Bill had a warehouse full of it.

One day a customer asked Bill what he thought of the taste of New Coke.

Bill replied, "I hate it."

How refreshing.

Bill gave his honest opinion regardless of what it would cost him financially.

For the person on the street who had no vested interest in New Coke's success to say they hated the taste was one thing, but to hear it from a man who had a warehouse full of it was quite another.

The negative opinion of the taste of New Coke quickly created a panic run in the original formula version of Coke.

It was in low supply, and the company stated they were not going to make any more.

Original Coca-Cola was like gold.

Wholesalers were calling Bill, offering to buy all of his inventory of original Coke at prices much higher than those offered for sale to his customers.

He didn't sell one case to any wholesaler.

He kept it all for his customers.

And he sold it at its original price.

Bill didn't gouge any frenzied customer looking for the original Coke, he sold whatever he had, whenever he had it.

He could have just pretended he didn't have anymore cases, as passing time would have only made those cases more valuable.

He didn't.

Some might call him a bad business man, as some of his partners in other stores were getting much higher prices for their cases. They decided to sell only half of what they had in inventory, and save the other half for when prices skyrocketed even more.

Looking back at this now, I would say Bill was a business man for the people.

Doing what was right for his customers always came before doing what was profitable for himself.

And by doing so he became beloved.

People define being rich in a narrow way they count the money one has.

They never look to see how one acquired the money.

If the definition of being rich was to count one's worth to their community, Bill was rich.

The outcry about the taste of New Coke was so bad that on July 11, 1985 Coca-Cola held a press conference to officially announce the return of original Coke, and to admit they had made a mistake.

The supply of the old version of Coke would be replenished.

The price of the original Coca-Cola immediately dropped all over the Island.

In Peconic Beverage it stayed the same price as it had been for the last 77 days.

The original price.

Some people call New Coke the worst mistake in the history of marketing.

But there are a few who believe it was the greatest ploy in the history of marketing.

The data supports the latter.

When Original Coke was reinstated, sales jumped 5%.

For years they were declining and Pepsi was catching up.

Now Coke was pulling away from Pepsi again.

By taking away their beloved Coke all together, people realized how much they really loved it.

A brilliant marketing plan.

Life is the same way.

Sometimes life takes away something we have grown accustomed to and in its absence we realize how much we really loved it.

There are life changing events that happen that take away life as we once knew it, and by doing so make us realize just how much we loved the original version of life.

Even though at times we thought we didn't.

Sometimes you don't realize how much you love something until it is gone.

Those lucky enough to get their original version of their life back after a life changing event, truly recognize life's great plan.

- 24 -
Old Naked Lady

What light is to the eyes
What love is to the heart
Freedom is to the soul.

Robert Green Ingersol

It was a real hot day.

A scorcher.

Just as the flow of the customers came to a trickle, in walks a ninety-year-old lady wearing a tube top.

Above her breasts.

I don't know if she was so hot that she was trying to cool off or if she was just so old that she didn't realize when she got dressed in the morning that she had placed the tube top above her breasts.

I really don't know.

What I did know was the old lady came to the counter and said, "Son, please bare with me because I am old," and she started asking for my help with an order.

"Bare with you – you are old?" I recounted the old lady's words in my head.

 "You are also naked." I said to myself.

I stood there stunned.

What should I do?

Do I tell her that her tube top was above her breasts?

Do I make believe this was normal attire?

Or do I do what any twenty-year-old would do and hold in my laughter and go tell his boss there is someone up front who wants to see him?

"Hey Bill, there's a customer that's looking for you in the front of the store," I called out as I ran to the back of the store.

Good times.

- 25 -
The Gravity of Life

If only it were possible for us to see
Farther than our knowledge reaches,
And even a little past
Than the far reaches of our foresight,
Perhaps we would endure our sorrows
With greater trust than our joys.

Rainer Marie Rilke
Letters To A Young Poet

Life can be so cruel.

We watched the rocket go up.

Then we watched it blow up.

Live on national TV.

On board were 6 astronauts and a school teacher named Christie McAullife.

You work all of your life trying to acquire something and it turns out that this something is the one thing that winds up killing you.

I remember Bill asking, "I wonder what's going through the minds of the people who weren't chosen for the mission?"

We all felt very bad for a long while.

Our lives even stood still - momentarily.
And then - life went on.

We weren't bad people.

That's just how life is.

A person who has just experienced a horrible event in their lives initially feels the world should stop spinning for them.

Rightfully so.

They feel people should call and visit more often.

People probably should.

But the world doesn't stop spinning, and people's own lives need their attention.

So life goes on.

I only wished there was a way people who have had a tragic thing happen to them could tell that other people were thinking of them.

Because they are.

All the time.

It is just not communicated.

That is the real shame.

Life is beyond comprehension.

Sometimes when we feel we are catching our biggest break, it may actually be a path to our demise.

Other times when we feel we are on our way to our demise, we catch our biggest break.

Life ebbs as we flow, and flows as we ebb.

One can never quite figure out why something happens.

One just has to trust that they are exactly where they are supposed to be at this exact moment in time.

To realize as long as you have a heart, you have a chance.

I don't mean a heart that is physically working, I mean one that is emotionally working.

A heart which is filled with love, desire and belief.

That heart.

Life, no matter how unexpected it may have turned out, no matter where you may be, no matter how much work is ahead to get to where you want to go, exists in your heart.

Don't just exist, live.

Today.

Be present today.

Right here.

And you will get there.

There.

Sometimes you get "there" by your own vision, but this is rare.

Often you get "there" by correcting a series of mistakes, each of which, if taken by themselves, would have taken you further off course. But somehow taken in their entirety directed you toward your intended destination.

Getting "there" this way is common, but not easy.

Sometimes you get "there" by the relentless pursuit of a loved one.

This is special.

However you get "there" is not the question.

Just get "there".

"There" - is exactly where you are meant to be.

On the way to "there" - is who you will become.

Why you are.

At every moment in your life, you are exactly where you are meant to be so you can become the person who you were meant to be.

So there - is here.

Right here, right now, is there.

By being present for all of the "here's" will surely get you "there".

The journey to get "there" is to be here.

No matter where "here" is.

- 26 -
ASS BACKWARDS AND
THE ONE EYED GUY

We are not in the coffee business
Serving people
But rather
We are in the people business
Selling coffee.

Howard Schultz
Starbucks

The shelf life of a person working in retail is less than the life expectancy of a bar-b-que left outside unprotected for the winter.

Working in retail can drive one crazy.

It took a few years, but it started to have a negative affect on my attitude.

All I knew was I wanted to be 'there', and not 'here' at my job.

I don't know where 'there' was, just that it wasn't 'here'.

Here, was boring, monotonous, predictable, mundane.

It felt like every day was Deja-vu, all over again, as Yogi would say.

The same people buying the same items at the same times each day, over and over again.

At 9:30 am I would open the store with a line of people at the door ready to return their empties.

At precisely 11:11, Ass Backwards (we called her Ass Backwards because it looked like this lady's ass was on backwards, as if someone somehow rotated it from the back of her body to the front) would come in for her single can of soda.

Exactly 33 seconds later she would be followed by the One Eyed Guy.

Shaky Ray would make his appearance at his exact time 12:02 pm.

And so on.

And so on.

And so on.

Every day.

The predictability drove me crazy.

Waiting on the same people who bought the same items, who bantered with you the exact same way – every day.

Day in and day out.

Bill recognized my change in perception of the world, and he knew I was deteriorating fast.

"Be grateful these people choose to come into the store every day. They are the ones who pay our salaries," Bill reminded me.

Not coincidentally the "John, you've got to find your passion" talks began at the same time.

Bill never held me back.

Actually he inspired me to find my passion so I could eventually move on.

Not because I was no longer a good worker but because he knew it was time.

- 27 -
WHEN YOUR LIGHT GOES OUT

Do not let your fire go out,
Spark by irreplaceable spark
In the hopeless swamps
Of the not-quite, the not-yet, and the not-at-all.
Do not let the hero in your soul
Perish in lonely frustration
For the life you deserved
And have never been able to reach.
The world you desire can be won.
It exists..
It is real..
It is possible..
It is yours.

Ayn Rand
Atlas Shrugged

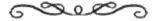

At Peconic Beverage virtually all the money was made during the summer.

The winter was the famine.

During one extremely slow winter I saw an opportunity for the store to make some money.

Every Friday night there was this one customer who came into the store, and before buying his six pack of beer, he stared at the St. Paulie Girl neon light that hung up above the beer cooler.

That is when the passion Bill was talking about first started to appear.

I just knew I had entrepreneurial blood.
One Friday afternoon I called Bill at home with an idea about my being able to generate some profit for the store during the winter months.

I asked him, "Everything in the store is for sale, right?"

He replied, "Yes", very slowly as if he was scouring his mind for anything he wouldn't want me to sell.

I said "OK."

That night when the "St. Paulie Girl" admirer came in for his weekly six pack and to stare at the St. Paulie Girl light, I went to work on my first entrepreneurial venture.

"That St. Paulie Girl neon light would look great in your man-cave," I said.

"Yea, it would. I've never seen one quite like it before. Is it for sale?"

"Everything in the store is for sale, but people just don't realize that. You can't get one of those in a store. We got it directly from the St. Paulie Girl distributors."

"How much do you want for it?"

"That light is very hard to get. I've never seen one anywhere else."

"How about $250?"

"Have you noticed how the neon shines around the St. Paulie Girl? That would look great in the dark."

"$300?"

"My boss doesn't really want to sell it, it's one of his favorites."

"How about $500?"

"All right. I guess at that price he would let it go."

"Bill, we had a good day today, one of the most profitable winter days that I can remember."

"The store was busy today?" Bill asked.

"Totally dead." I said.

"Then how did we have one of our best winter days ever?"

"I sold the St. Paulie Girl neon sign for $500."

"You did what? We got that sign from the distributor for free," Bill said.

"I know, and the best part is they are willing to give us a replacement for free."

"If you ask them for a replacement it must be for a completely different decoration," Bill said.

"That is even better – an endless inventory of new items to sell." I said.

And that winter, for the next eight Friday nights, I sold a different neon beer decoration light for $500 to the same customer.

He was ecstatic.

His basement bar looked great decorated in hard to get neon lights from every beer manufacturer in the country.

And the store was a bit more profitable during the winter.

Sounds like a win-win all around.

After each sale, Bill offered me the $500 but I didn't take a single dollar of any of the sales.

I was paid in a different way.

I found my passion.

I became an Entrepreneur for life.

The ability to turn nothing into something.

- 28 -
TONIC WATER LADY

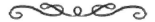

No one can make you feel inferior,
Without your consent.

Eleanor Roosevelt
This Is My Story

"Young man, I need a bottle of tonic, three bottles of seltzer in the small bottles, I hate the large bottles, a case of Evian and seven bottles of Heineken," a prissy lady in a yellow dress wearing a white hat and white gloves on a hot summer day.

"The bottle of tonic can be found on that wall over there, the seltzer is over there and…" I started saying before Bill interrupted me.

"John, I'll take over from here."

"Tonic Water Lady" would be the last customer I would ever wait on at Peconic Beverage.

Retail had been slowly taking its toll on me.

"Tonic Water Lady's" upper class snobbishness accelerated my retail intolerance.

"Hey, what happened back there?" Bill asked after "Tonic Water Lady" had left.

"She actually wanted me to get her the tonic water off of the shelf, then go get her some seltzer..." I fumed.

"She thinks she's better than me." I said.

"Nobody can make you feel like they are better than you unless you let them. And right now you are letting them." Bill said.

"John, I see how you watch FNN on TV, I see how you sold those neon signs, and you're great with numbers. You should become a stockbroker."

So I did.

- 29 -
THE MILLISECOND OF TRUTH

All my instincts,
They return
And the grand facade,
So soon will burn

Peter Gabriel
In Your Eyes

There is a millisecond of time when the truth is flashed in plain sight for all to see.

It is in one's eyes when you share good news with a person, it is in one's voice during an initial greeting, it is in ones' aura when you are in their presence.

For a millisecond, a window of truth into one's soul will exist after which it will be quite deceptively adjusted and camouflaged into anything but the truth.

The millisecond of truth is always present.

It is infallible.

Ignore it at your own peril.

I first saw the millisecond of truth in Bill's eyes.

I had taken Bill's advice.

In October of 1986, on the same day Billy Hatcher crushed Met fans hearts with his 16th inning single to win game 6 of the National League Championship Series, I became a stockbroker.

I remember things like that.

As a new stockbroker, it took many months, working long hours, but eventually I had some greater than expected financial success.

One day as I was on my way to a beach in the Hamptons, I stopped in at Peconic Beverage to visit with Bill.

We got to talking.

I told him a story of how I was laying on the beach the other day thinking to myself that "life can't get any better than this."

I had just purchased my dream car and house all in the last week.

That was when I first noticed the millisecond of truth.

In Bill's eyes.

Sincere happiness for my recent financial success.

That is what flashed in his eyes for the briefest of seconds and then it was gone.

Even good emotions get adjusted after the original reaction; it is just the way the millisecond of truth works.

I have learned to trust this millisecond of truth more than anything in the world.

I trust it over what someone says and over what someone promises to do.

For it is the truest truth there is.

- 30 -
YOU CAN'T KEEP A GOOD MAN DOWN

In prosperity,
Our friends know us.
In adversity,
We know our friends.

G.K. Chesterton

Six years passed until the next time I saw Bill.

We ran into each other at a mutual friends wedding.

Bill asked how I was doing.

I replied that my life couldn't get any worse.

And there it was again.

For the second time in my life I saw the millisecond of truth.

This time the millisecond of truth revealed to me sincere sadness.

Bill was extremely upset to hear me say that.

We talked about how much had changed for me since the last time we saw each other.

In six years my life went from: "My life can't get any better than this" to "I don't know how my life can get any worse."

How did that happen?

Quite simply, I had changed my original formula on how to live life.

Randy Pausch, in his book "The Last Lecture" tells a story of pouring a can of soda on the white leather seats of his brand new Volkswagen Cabrio to show his niece and nephew that "People are more important than things."

Let's just say that during those six years my niece and nephew would never have had the chance to ride in my car because I would have been at work attempting to make more money.

Somewhere during those six years, I decided that my original formula for life was not working as well as it should have, and I decided to go with a New Formula.

My new formula for life was – More Money.
Money bought things.

Things I never had.

Things I wanted.

Things I got.

Even though there was nothing he could do to help my situation, Bill's eyes told me he was rooting for me.

"Don't worry, you'll recover. You can't keep a good man down."

It took some time, and I did recover.

By changing back to the original formula on how to live life.

The one I was exposed to by working with Bill.

People are more important than things, especially money.

Life has a funny way of taking away things to show you how much you really love people.

A brilliant marketing plan, I would say.

Part III

There are no weeds,
And no worthless men,
There are only bad farmers.

Victor Hugo
Les Miserables

- 31 -
Look on Your Stoop

If we will be quiet and ready enough
We will find compensation
For every disappointment.

Henry David Thoreau

Everyone has eyes, but how many people see with a vision?

Everyone has ears, but how many people truly listen?

Everyone has fingers, but how many people feel with every touch?

Everyone has a heart, but how many people have compassion?

Everyone has family, but how many people really feel a sense of belonging?

Yes, adversity takes things from you which you don't want to give up, but it must replace what it takes with an equal or greater gift.

Those are just the rules.

The tricky part about adversity is that it doesn't tell you the rules.

It is up to you to figure them out.

There are many gifts that remain unopened in our lives.

They have been delivered by adversity.

Most remain on our stoop just like when the UPS man delivers a package, doesn't ring the doorbell and just walks away without letting us know that something special has been delivered.

Eventually we realize that there is a special package waiting to be opened and we go looking for it.

Go look on your stoop, look on the back porch or near the garage - I bet there are a lot of special packages waiting to be opened.

Open them.

- 32 -
THE LOVELESS PRISON

Stone walls do not a prison make,
Nor iron bars a cage;
If I have freedom in my love
And in my soul am free,
Angels alone, that soar above,
Enjoy such liberty.

Richard Lovelace
To Althea, From Prison

It's an unfortunate but true statement that we all have people in our lives we've given up on.

People we once cared for deeply, people who once brought value to our lives, people who have wronged us or someone else… in our eyes.

Wronged someone so badly that we do not even try to reconcile, it is just easier to disassociate, abandon ship and move on.

Lovers, friends, kids, family members – people we know to be good people, but who have done something we just can't reconcile with… in our mind.

So instead, we decide to put these people in our own little prison.

A prison that does not take away their freedom, but one which cuts off our love to them.

This is the worst prison of all.
The 'loveless prison'.

There are 2.2 million people incarcerated in the United States.

There are exponentially more in 'loveless prisons' nationwide.

These 'loveless prisons', the ones in which we are the sole person on the parole board, do not rehabilitate a man.

It hardens them.

I don't see how withholding love will ever make any situation better.

The answer is always more love. Not less.

- 33 -
DON'T LET THE LIE WIN

Any time fear and worry
Come knocking on my door
Trying to barge in
They are going to have to hang out with
Faith, hope and trust.
And they are not going to
Let them hang out long.

Ernie Johnson
TNT Basketball Analyst

Two of my all time favorite books are:
"Every Second Counts" and "It's Not About the Bike",
both written by Lance Armstrong.

I have read each of them many times.

Any time I refer to either, I undoubtedly learn something new about the human spirit.

Both books are about Lance Armstrong's fight and struggle to beat cancer, and then going on to win five Tour De Force cycling events, the athletic event thought to be one of the most physically and mentally grueling in the world.

I am very fortunate that I have never had the experience of fighting to overcome cancer, but I found both books to be extremely inspirational.

So did the cancer community.

Both Lance Armstrong and his two books provided belief, hope and inspiration to so many people – people who are in the fight of their lives.

I am certain the books had a great impact on improving the quality of life of many others.

Then it was revealed that Lance Armstrong had lied about taking performance-enhancing drugs during each of his Tour de Force victories.

Everyone immediately put Lance Armstrong into the 'loveless prison'.

I, myself, did the same.

Everything he ever said or stood for became a lie.

Belief, hope and inspiration ... pulled from the people who needed it the most, at the time they needed it the most.

As I write this, neither of his books is for sale on any venue.

That is so unfortunate.

But I understand.

How can one be inspired by a lie?

For a very long time I felt the same way, and didn't refer to his books.

I threw out all of his redeeming qualities because he did something wrong, something terribly wrong.

In essence, I let the lie win.

I just should have listened to Lance Armstrong's own hint he gave to everyone when he titled his book: "It's not about the bike."

It is about the belief.

It is about the hope.

It is about the inspiration.

Winning the Tour De Force five times pales in comparison to offering belief, hope and inspiration to millions of people who are in the fight of their lives against cancer.

Eventually Lance Armstrong was stripped of all his Tour De Force victories.

But sadder still, millions of people were stripped of their belief, hope and inspiration during the biggest fight of their lives.

Instead of isolating Lance Armstrong's lie and not believing in any of his cycling success, the world threw out all of Lance Armstrong, including all of his redeeming qualities of belief, hope and inspiration in his personal fight to overcome cancer.

It took me a while, but I recently was able to separate in my mind, Lance Armstrong the cancer survivor, from Lance Armstrong the cyclist.

I started to refer to his books again, and I'm so glad I did.

There are so many great parts to each of his books.

Parts which are unavailable elsewhere - his approach, his attitude, his change as a man after adversity struck, and his new perspective on life, all of which make a great inspiring read.

I am glad I started referring to them again.

During our lifetime, we will all run into our own personal Lance Armstrong.

I would advise you to believe in them anyway.

Because "Every Second Counts" and "It's Not About the Bike".

It's about the belief, hope and inspiration one can impart to others – attributes that can improve the quality of other people's lives during the time they need it the most.

- 34 -
A D.I.M.E. IS WORTHLESS

Never believe a prediction
That doesn't empower you.

Sean Stephenson

A few years back, when someone I knew and valued in my life wronged me in some way, I D.I.M.E'd them.

D.I.M.E. - Dead In My Eyes.

I put them in a mental prison, withdrew my love and support and couldn't care less if they withered away or not.

You wronged me – I D.I.M.E you.

This act became easier and easier for me to do.

In the beginning, my life became less complicated.
I didn't have to deal with any nonsense – just send anyone who wronged me to my mental prison and the situation was handled.

Until one day, after a few years, I realized I had imprisoned almost everyone I knew in my life, and

I had mentally imprisoned some quality people along the way.

I had thrown out their redeeming qualities in the process.

My mental 'loveless prison' was full.

My life was empty.

Just like when I knew I needed to separate Lance Armstrong's qualities and be able to again refer to "It's Not About the Bike" and "Every Second Counts," I knew I had to start releasing my friends, family and acquaintances from my mental 'loveless prison'.

It was easy. I had the master key.

Love.

Once I re-instilled love to the people I had mentally imprisoned, my life improved dramatically.

My world seemed full again.
I believe life is about belief and love.

Decide whose team you're on, never lose belief, and always love.

No matter what.
It is that simple.

- 35 -
Separation of Act and Person

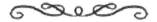

What a slut time is.
She screws everybody.

John Green
The Fault in our Stars

I have learned to separate bad acts from good people.

I have learned to realize people are human.

They are going to mess up.

Sometimes they are going to mess up in a big way.

They are going to wrong someone or even you.

Sometimes they will wrong you many times.

They are going to let you down.

Sometimes, they will even try to hold you down.

As Mother Teresa said: "Believe in them and love them anyway."

I believe when you truly know a person is a good person, it is important to never give up on them.

Ever.

Remember, "It's not about the bike."

It's not about the mistake that was made.

It is about focusing on the good.

It is about focusing on the belief and the love.

It is about focusing on the people in our lives.

We all have a very limited time on this earth.

And every second counts.

That part, Lance Armstrong did not lie about.

- 36 -
Angels on a Train

I need a sign
To let me know your here.
Cause my TV set keeps it all from being clear.
I want a reason
For the way things have to be.
I need a hand
To help build up some hope inside of me.

Calling All Angels
Train

People will come in and out of your life like passengers traveling on a train.

And it always seems like everyone is traveling to the same destination as you are.

Until you realize they are not.

Everyone is on his or her own journey.

People can and will get off the train at any stop.

There will be a few people in your life that will make the whole trip with you, who believe in you, accept that you are human and understand that mistakes will be made along the way, and that you will get to your desired destination together - no matter what.

Be very grateful for these people, for they are rare.

When you find one, don't ever let go.

Be very wary of people sneaking on at certain stops when things are going well and acting like they have been there for the whole ride.

For they will be the first to depart.

There will be people who secretly try to get off the ride, and there will be those that very publicly will jump off.

Don't pay any heed to the defectors.

Just know where and how people get off is more of a reflection on them, than it is on you.

Be blessed for the ones who get on at the worst stops when everyone else is departing.

For they are special.

Always hold them dear to your heart.

For they are the important ones.

Embrace them.

Welcome them.

Pay close attention to them.

They are there to make sure you complete your journey and arrive at your destination.

And when you do, you will look up to smile at them, to thank them…

And they will be gone.

For their job will have been done.

For they are not defectors - they are angels.

Just know a piece of them will remain with you forever.

If you ever have the opportunity to be that person who has a chance to walk into someone's life when everyone else is walking out, embrace it, relish it.

For it is one of the most important roles you can have in someone else's life - to be their angel.

PART IV

No experience really goes wasted.
True understanding
Is to see the events of life in this way.
Truly whatever arises in life
Is the right material to bring about your growth
And the growth of those around you.
Everything contains some special purpose
And a hidden blessing.
All of life is here
To greet you old and faithful friend.

Marcus Aerealius

- 37 -
MY WISH

The harder the conflict,
The more glorious the triumph.
What we obtain too cheap,
We esteem too lightly.
It is dearness only
That gives everything its value.

Thomas Paine

There is a sweet spot in becoming a member of the "Life Changing Events Club."

There has to be just the right amount of pain and hurt caused by the event in your life that introduces you to the club.

"Too little" pain and hurt, where one forgets and reverts back to their original life without gaining proper perspective to fully appreciate life is pointless.

"Too harsh" pain and hurt, where one's will is broken, will destroy one's outlook on life and make that person useless.

It has to be just enough pain and suffering that makes one change their perspective on life while still being able to move forward and live, unwilling to ever let go of the pain and suffering, realizing how important it is to one's perspective.

That is just the right amount.

Pain and suffering when channeled become perspective.

Perspective leads to gratitude.

And gratitude is what helps the world become a better place.

I hope beyond hope that Bill receives just the right amount of pain and suffering for his actions, so he has permanent perspective on life.

Which will give him permanent gratitude as well.
For he is a good man - who still has a lot of good to give to this world.

A world that so badly needs it.

- 38 -
Three Wishes

No one can build you the bridge
On which you,
And only you,
Must cross the river of life.

Friedrich Nietzsche

We all go through a period in our lives when we feel we are not where we should be.

The funny thing is, it is exactly where we need to be.

Coming out of high school in 1983, I envisioned myself doing so much more than working at a beverage center while commuting to college.

Looking back, if I had to compare the value of what I learned working at Peconic Beverage to what I learned at college, the comparison wouldn't even be close.

I learned more about life working with Bill than I ever learned anywhere else.

People are more important than things.

Some thirty-two years later, my son is in a similar situation as I was when I got out of high school.

He is not exactly where he thought he would be at this point in his life.

I smile.

I know it is where he needs to be.

I only wish, with my second wish, that he will run into his own Bill during this time in his life.

A good man who will teach him what life is all about.

People.

As for my third wish – I would like to offer it back to the universe so it can use it however it seems fit.

It seems to have a brilliant plan.

- 39 -
Silent Whispers

If I were to wish for anything,
I should not wish for wealth or power,
But for an eye that sees the possible.

Soren Kierkegaard

At a commencement address John Green recently gave he asked all the people in the audience to sit in silence and think about the people in their lives who made that moment possible.

He then said to the audience, "Let me submit to you that this is the definition of a good life. You want to be the kind of person other people will think about in their own silence."

I realize that it was silence that whispered Bill's name in my ear.

Although it had always been in my heart.

-40-
WHOLE LIVES

We are all ordinary people,
But even an ordinary secretary,
Or a housewife,
Or a teenager,
Can within their own small ways
Turn on a small light
In a dark room.

Miep Gies
The woman who helped hide Anne Frank

I open the inside cover of one book and I write:

Bill,

I want you to know you are a good man.

I am thinking of you and your family.

Your friend,

JohnA Passaro

I place the book in a bubble mailer, address it to the State Penitentiary and I drop it off at the post office.

On the way home I pass a Whole Foods store.

And I smile.

It has taken me all of my life to realize my goal in life is not to look successful to the world but to be significant to a few.

A good man taught me that.

WWW.JOHNAPASSARO.COM

THANK YOU FOR READING

"A GOOD MAN"

JohnA Passaro

WWW.JOHNAPASSARO.COM

ALL BOOKS BY JOHNA PASSARO

www.JOHNAPASSARO

Every Breath is Gold – The Complete Series

6 Minutes Wrestling with Life (Book 1)

Again (Book 2)

Your Soul Knows (Book 3)

A Good Man

WWW.JOHNAPASSARO.COM

Contact Info

My greatest joy of writing comes from the people I have met who have reached out to me and have shared their life stories with me.

I cherish every email I receive.

I encourage you to contact me.

Email - johnapassaro@icloud.com

Like me on Facebook -

Follow me on Twitter - @johnapassaro

Webpage – www.johnapassaro.com

WWW.JOHNAPASSARO.COM

COULD I ASK YOU FOR A FAVOR?

The greatest compliment that a reader can pay a writer is
to tell a friend about their book.
I would be honored if you were able to do so.

Word of mouth
The simplest way to find great books to read is when
friends share their reading experiences with each other
by word of mouth.

Book reviews
If you feel this book has touched you in a small way, or
has stirred emotions inside of you that have given you a
different perspective on life, I invite for you to leave a
book review on the site that you purchased this book.
This will allow potential readers to understand the book
is worth the investment of their money and time.
The Book Review doesn't need to be perfect; it just needs
to be something from you, letting other readers know
how you feel about this book.

Social Media
Please share your reading experience with your friends
on your Facebook and Twitter social media pages. I
thank you in advance, as all communication to your
family and friends is greatly appreciated.

WWW.JOHNAPASSARO.COM

Made in the USA
Middletown, DE
28 October 2015